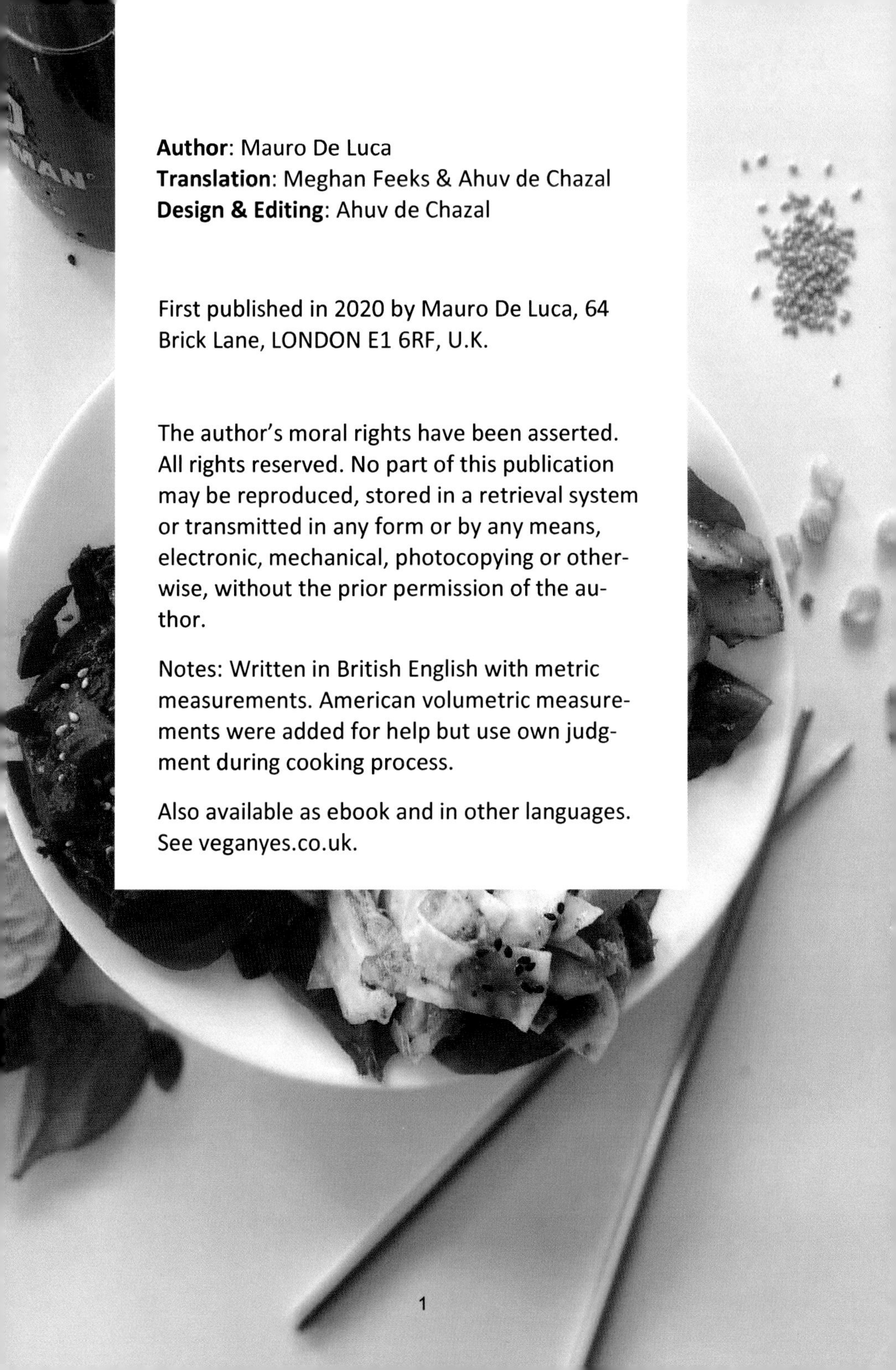

Author: Mauro De Luca
Translation: Meghan Feeks & Ahuv de Chazal
Design & Editing: Ahuv de Chazal

First published in 2020 by Mauro De Luca, 64 Brick Lane, LONDON E1 6RF, U.K.

Notes: Written in British English with metric measurements. American volumetric measurements were added for help but use own judgment during cooking process.

Also available as ebook and in other languages. See veganyes.co.uk.

CONTENTS

FOREWORD

Science and modern society is only just waking up to the sheer importance of gut health and its vast effect on our physical and mental health. Now described as the second brain, our digestive system is a complicated system made up of organs I still can't name, bodily functions we all know but prefer not to talk about and most importantly, a gazillion bacteria and microorganisms living within us that aren't human. Scary concepts but the likes of Yacult or other probiotic yogurt products can be credited in making us aware that good gut bacteria are a useful, not a scary thing.

Like most people, I didn't care about these things until my body forced me to confront it: Constant stomach cramps, indigestion, smelly farts and my doctor telling me I have "IBS" changed this. *Irritable Bowel Syndrome* was the diagnosis, but I was not told what to specifically do and for the first time there was no quick fix solution from a health care system that has sold me the idea that we just need to pop pills to continue functioning like machines.

In retrospect, my body was telling me that my environment, habits and diet weren't good enough for it to function well. Plus other things I wasn't directly responsible for like antibacterial chemicals around us everywhere, antibiotics given without warnings and pesticide-rich, monoculturally grown food devoid of things from mother nature science knows little about to this day.

Whatever it is that modern life is harming our gut bacteria balance, I learnt that cultures across the globe invented probiotic foods that introduce bacteria into our digestive tracts and help us maintain a balance. Our ancestors maybe didn't know the science behind it but by pickling and fermenting foods prior to the invention of fridges and preservatives, they did their bellies a massive favour. Now in the age of antibac gels, maybe these live-culture foods are more important than ever: Be that kefir, yogurt, kombucha, sauerkraut, sour pickles, tempeh, miso or my firm favourite: kimchi, the ingredient this book is dedicated to. I was thus honoured to help translate, edit, design and publish the recipes of Chef Mauro that incorporate this superfood into a creative variety of dishes. I hope you will find new favourite recipes to introduce into your weekly cooking routines so that you to may realise the benefits of looking after your gut health, whatever your age.

Ahuv de Chazal
EDITOR

INTRODUCTION

If you had told me when I was a small boy growing up in Tuscany that one day, I would be a chef, running a restaurant in London that specialised in vegan Korean-Italian fusion cuisine, I never would have believed you.

For starters, it wasn't until recently that I thought of myself as a chef at all, even if I always had an interest in cooking. Secondly, I had no idea what 'vegan' meant — or why anyone would choose to be one. Finally, I wouldn't have been able to point to Korea or even Asia on a map, even in early adulthood. Geography was never my strong suit.

In sum, I would have thought the whole idea of becoming a vegan Korean-Italian fusion chef was *pura pazzia*. Pure craziness. And I admit that, in a way, it is!

Looking back, however, I can also see that this is always what I was meant to do. And having long struggled to find my path in life, I now realize that, in many ways, I've been on this path all along.

Writing this book is an extension of this path, for while cooking is my craft, my true passion is sharing the happiness and fulfilment it gives me with others. I am thus bringing my recipes beyond my cosy Brick Lane eatery to kitchen around the world and to you,

Ciao

Mauro

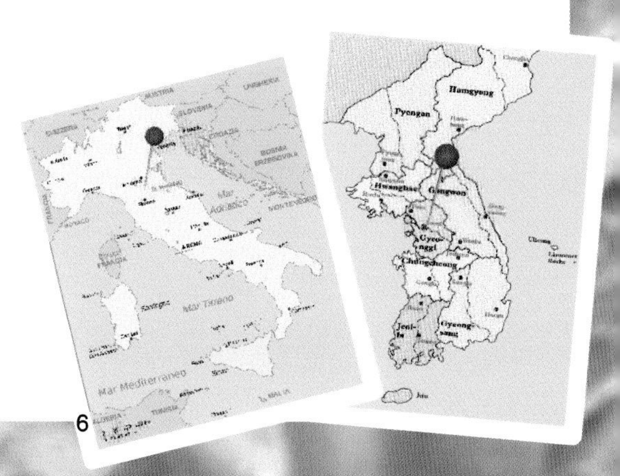

MY STORY

I've always had a thing for kitchens. Even as a toddler, I loved playing with my cousin Francesca's kitchen set, with all its toy pots, pans and utensils. We would concoct dishes made with dirt and leaves, and it gave us great pride to serve them to our parents.

From that point on, I spent as much time as I could in the kitchen gathering ingredients and knowledge. I remember watching my grandmother Maria who made lasagna every Sunday. I also remember collecting little fish that the fishermen would discard along the seashore in Summer, to then prepare a delicious soup that I shared with my family.

But the person who taught me most about the creative joys of cooking was my mother, who rarely ventured further than our refrigerator to make a tasty meal out of whatever happened to be in there. I was so intrigued by this magic that as a young man, I often told my parents I wouldn't be home for dinner, just so I could return after they'd eaten to prepare a meal for myself. Like my mother, I would start with no plans, no particular recipes in mind. I would simply make do with whatever I could find, using only my hands and my creativity.

Some years later, I started to realize that cooking was not just an interest, but a passion. I was spending New Year's at my friend Massimo's home, a beautiful villa in Chianti with breath-taking views of Florence. In the early afternoon, we started preparing dinner in his fancy kitchen, with sharp knives, shiny appliances and drawers that hid useful shelves. We felt like kids at a carnival, free to go on as many rides as we wanted, making jokes and expressing our emotions with light and happy hearts.

Cooking gives me this thrill by combining two of the greatest joys in life: the joy of creating something, and the joy of sharing these creations with others. The beauty of sharing cooking is that its transformative powers don't stop with the meal, for dinners have the power to change hearts, minds and history.

I have experienced this power first hand: it was over a dinner in Florence that I met a beautiful Korean woman named Min, and my life (and cooking) were transformed forever.

A KOREAN-ITALIAN LOVE AFFAIR

Min is now my wife and the love of my life, and she opened my eyes to new ways of cooking and thinking about food. A doctor of Asian medicine, she introduced me to the idea of *qi*, the vital energy that flows through all living things. In our bodies, *qi* circulates through channels, called meridians, which connect the various organs and bodily functions through energy points known as *chakras*.

Health arises when our chakras are aligned and *qi* flows freely through our meridians, but blockages result in poor health. In the ancient Asian tradition, food is thought of as medicine that can unblock qi and restore balance to the chakras. At Vegan Yes, Min advises on the ingredients and products we use to maximise the health and energetic benefits of everything we serve.

Anyone who has visited our restaurant in London will know that a key ingredient in our dishes is kimchi, or Korean pickled vegetables, in a variety of brilliant colours. Now recognized as a superfood, kimchi is bursting with benefits, including fibre and beneficial microbes that promote gut health and immune function.

Family and community are also central to both the Korean and Italian culinary traditions. The way we sit at the table and eat our food is different: for example, eating whilst lifting your elbows is considered impolite in Italy, but accepted and indeed necessary in Korea, where you sit on the floor with your legs in front of you at a low table.

In Korea, it is also normal to pick up your bowl to drink the broth when you have finished your noodles. In Italy, your mother would smack you for this.

Whatever these differences, though, love, family and sharing are at the heart of both traditions. And as the barriers that separated my world view fell away, so too did the barriers in my cooking: kimchi found its way into lasagna. Olive oil found true love with soya sauce. And my special version of Korean-Italian fusion cuisine was born!

GETTING BACK TO MY (VEGETABLE) ROOTS

Another notable element of my cuisine is that it's vegan. In some ways, my path to a vegan diet was accidental: after struggling with poor health and digestive problems, I experimented with eliminating one type of food at a time over the course of ten years, and by the time I felt better, I realised I had become a vegan.

In other ways, though, I believe my arrival at a plant-based diet was destiny, for it brought me full circle back to where my culinary journey started — to my family home in the Tuscan countryside. There, my beloved grandfather Giuseppe could often be found in his garden, munching on the variety of vegetables he grew there. Every day for lunch and dinner, he delighted in eating a big bowl of raw vegetables, like a child eating ice cream. The second course could vary from a spoonful of soup in the evening, a forkful of pasta at lunch, or perhaps a bite of chicken or fresh mozzarella. But fresh vegetables were the mainstay of his diet, and he was strong, energetic and sharp until his death at more than 100 years old.

The story of my cooking is thus the story of a 360-degree journey that started and ended with my childhood in Italy — but when I returned, I brought with me all I'd learned from my explorations of love, life, health and different cultures. In 2015, the journey continued with the opening of our restaurant, Vegan Yes, on the famously multi-cultural Brick Lane in London

Now, with the publication of Kimchi Soo,
I am inviting you to join me on my journey by trying out
some of my recipes in your own home and thank you for joining me
on my crazy adventures.

Buon appetito

식사를 즐기십시오

REVOLUTIONARY STYLE

The first important thing to understand is to open your mind to a FUSION kitchen, giving you the opportunity to use ingredients from all over the world. Some nationalities have a very strong culinary culture so it is difficult to change these within ourselves. In this book I propose new and different methods from those you may know, in order to cook healthy and energising food beyond a single cultural boundary.

RAW OIL

Not everyone knows that when fats and oils are used at high temperatures their molecular structure changes, suffering a lot of damage, the temperature determines a series of chemical reactions responsible for the molecular genesis of food until they become harmful to health carcinogens.

I believe that in light of this information, it is even more important to choose a variety of oils in which there are stable fats, that is, they don't deteriorate with cooking at high temperatures. To ensure that the variety of oil chosen is not harmful it is necessary to check what its smoke point is and when oil becomes rancid.

So, comparing all oils it becomes clear that based on these criteria of degradation, the winners are extra virgin olive oil and coconut oil.

However, a study has shown that a meal with heated olive oil increases the markers of oxidation as opposed to when raw, uncooked extra virgin olive oil is used.

Furthermore, heating oil can damage some of its antioxidants and Vitamin E, which are sensitive to heat. For that reason, I no longer heat oils in any form.

You might wonder how I get by in cooking a variety of dishes without ever using heated oil. You will see how this is possible with the recipes in this book which includes an example of how to roast tofu in a pan without using oil.

I feel that when people fry ingredients at the start of preparing their meal, they do so because that's just how we have been taught. However, in so many dishes you then add wet ingredients, like adding tomatoes to fried onions. The taste of the few droplets of oil from the fried onions then gets lost swimming in the wide ocean of the tomato sauce as you cook the meal for another 20-30 minutes. You may as well have added the oil afterwards in its raw form and saved yourself the carcinogenics.

So, I omit oil during the heating of my dishes but use it as a dressing at the end. It will be tastier and more nutritious for your body.

TEMPERATURE

Hot and cold: cooked or raw?

The energetic values within food changes according to how food is prepared.

Regardless of whether food is eaten raw or cooked, it is important to know food preparation affects nutrient absorption and digestibility.

Raw doesn't always mean better. Cooked food has its place in a healthy diet, especially when you take into account the energy level or health condition of your body.

Steaming, baking, frying, boiling and grilling affect the nutritional content of foods.

Subjected to too much heat, food can burn and become harmful to health, even a humble piece of toast can become a dangerous invader. Burning food brings toxic substances into the body which not only slow down digestive processes, but also favours the accumulation of toxins in the liver.

Yet even when food is cooked at high temperature and the burning is avoided, nutrients are being lost quickly.

According to Traditional Chinese Medicine, each food contains its own *qi*, or its vital energy, which in turn gives us nourishment and energy. When a food is "mistreated" with inadequate cooking, its *qi* is disturbed and diminished and what we introduce becomes a food that challenges the body rather than providing benefit.

For this reason, I decided to use low temperatures in my kitchen for cooking food, balancing flavour and nutrients.

Precautions

- avoid burning food because it is a source of toxins for the body
- include both raw and hot food in each meal
- always prefer cooking at low temperatures

Ideally cooking temperature does not exceed 42° at which the food can still be considered raw.

If proper heating is preferred, I prefer using a frying pan or the oven as these methods are the ones that allow you to retain the most nutrients of the food.

Boiling or stewing on the other hands disperses the nutrients quickly. If boiling is preferred, try to use little water and then drink the water as a soup since it will be rich in nutrients given off by the vegetables you boiled in it.

However, when your body is craving hot food, it's better to trust your intuition and go for cooked food.

MY INGREDIENTS

Now that you know the story behind my cuisine, I'd like to share a few words on some of the key ingredients you'll find in this book

Olive oil

The nectar of my existence. I won't go so far as to say my mother put it in my baby bottle, but I never go on vacation without it. Rich in nutrients and monounsaturated fat, it helps regulate cholesterol levels. It also contains oleic acid, which is important for cardiovascular health.

Chilli

From the testimony of archaeological finds we know that as early as 5500 BC spicy chilli was known in Mexico as a cultivated plant. Chili came to Europe thanks to Christopher Columbus who brought it from the Americas, most likely the species *Capsicum chinense*, of the Scotch Bonnet or Habanero varieties, the most common in those islands. Korean chilli flakes are known as Gochugaru and are small, dried, bright red flakes that add sweet flavour without too much heat, either in the cooking process or as a condiment. Buy online or at an Asian supermarket.

Kimchi

The first information on kimchi dates back to the Three Kingdoms period (37 BC)

The oldest form of kimchi was made from salted vegetables. From the twelfth century onwards, the recipe was enriched with spices, thus giving the kimchi different flavours (sweet and bitter) and colours (white and orange). Spicy chilli, another key ingredient of contemporary kimchi, was unknown to Koreans and was introduced only in the seventeenth century by traders coming from the west of Korea (probably via India).

Kimchi has since become part of the *Intangible Cultural Heritage of Humanity* as declared by UNESCO after both South and North Korea submitted a request in 2013 and 2015 respectively.

Soya sauce

Soya sauce originated originally in China, where fermented sauces have been known since ancient times, developing in the Zhou dynasty (1st century BCE). By the 3rd century CE historical Chinese texts noted that “the Goguryeo people (present day Korea) are good at brewing fermented soya beans”.

Originally, soya sauce was born as a fermented product based on the legume of the same name, among the nutritional qualities of the sauce stand out an antioxidant content 10 times greater than that of red wine and digestive properties. On the other hand, its salt content makes it unsuitable to people on low sodium diets.

Sesame

Sesame is a plant originating from India. It is an annual plant, grows erect to a height of one two meters, the fruits are capsule-shaped and are about two centimetres long and they contain numerous small seeds of various colours (from 50 to 100).

Sesame, thanks to its properties, is among the oldest condiments known. Already 5000 years ago it was cultivated in India since it was fundamental not only for human nutrition (ground and mixed in food) but also for its use as a fuel for lamps and for its medicinal, religious and cosmetic uses. Indians themselves attribute the origin of sesame to a gift granted by the deities: according to Indian literature, sesame seeds were born from the sweat drops of Vishnu.

The importance of sesame in Indian culture is reported not only in Ayurvedic Medicine as it stimulates digestion and cures urinary tract diseases such as dysmenorrhea and haemorrhoids, but also in Buddhist sacred texts it is in fact considered one of the superior foods (widely used in the monks' diet) and the Buddha remembered that "sesame seed, despite being very small, could generate a large tree".

The nutritional and medicinal value of this "little treasure" was also appreciated by the Egyptians until it was included in the Ebers papyrus (ca. 1550 BC) with the term *semsent* among the remedies against headache and bleeding.

Type "00" Flour

The double zero refers to specifically Italian milled flour that is used for pasta making. In Italian we pronounce it "doppio zero". The grading system four milled flours in Italy is 2, 1, 0 or 00 and indicates to how finely ground the flour is and how much of the bran and germ has been removed. "2" for example is a wholemeal flour while "00" is the most refined of the three and has the lowest level of bran. It is similar to unbleached all-purpose/plain flour, which is a mix of hard and soft wheat, and although finer, it creates a dough that is silkier and maintains a chewiness when the pasta is cooked due to the higher wheat protein (gluten) content.

CAPERS

Capers are the buds from a shrub growing in Italy and around the Mediterranean. They add a particular intense flavour, often departed from a salty brine or sour fermentation. They pack numerous flavonoids and thus are great antioxidant food. Capers have a positive effect on metabolism and can help against cholesterol.

They also are anti-inflammatory and antithrombotic, so helpful for those suffering from varicose veins and due to a flavonoid called "rutin".

Capers are the highest plant source of this particular flavonoid. It strengthens capillaries and helps to prevent blood clotting.

The tastiest capers to eat as an aperitif are the ones with a stem, like a cherry as they have a milder, sweeter taste.

Vegan

KIMCHI RED

빨간

Rosso

Our key probiotic ingredient

This is the most traditional way of making kimchi. Fish sauce is usually used in South Korea but this recipe, which I learnt from a North Korean I met in Hong Kong uses a fruit paste instead!

Ingredients

1.5kg (2) heads Chinese leaf
100g (1) small fresh carrot
25g (1.5 tbs) salt
10g (1 tbsp) capers
10g (3 tsp) garlic
10g (3 tsp) ginger roots
¼ honey melon
20g (1 oz) Korean chilli flakes
10g (3 tsp) rice powder
100ml (¼ cup + 3tbsp) water

Chinese leaf is also known as Napa Cabbage

Chinese leaf Preparation

Take the Chinese leaf and slice its green parts with a large knife into 3x3cm (1x1 inch) chunks (see top row)

Divide the white bottom into four parts (see bottom row), then chop these into match-stick shaped pieces. You want them to be much smaller than the green chunks because this part of the Chinese leaf is much firmer.

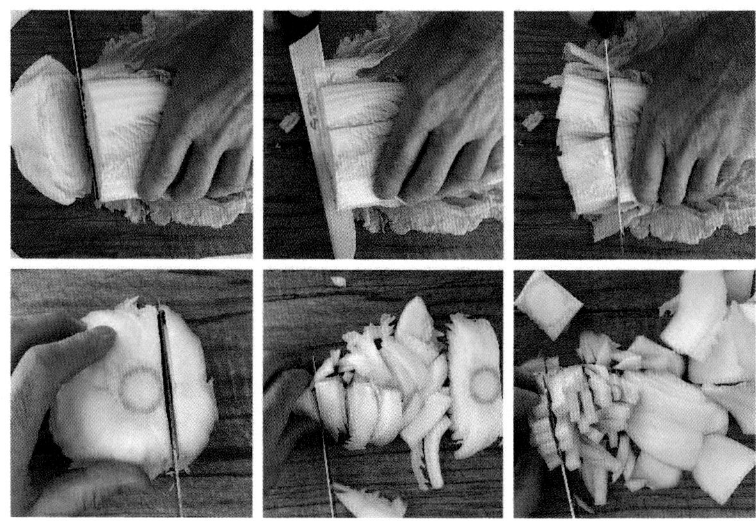

Put the chopped Chinese leaf in a bowl and add the salt. Mix with your hands.

Leave the Chinese leaf to sit for maximum 12 hours at room temperature.

After that time, the salt will have drawn quite a bit of liquid from the Chinese leaf. Drain it and squeeze the chunks to remove further liquid. Our YouTube video shows you what this may look like!

Rice cream

Take a sauce pot and put rice flour and ambient water in it. Heat mixture on the hob and keep stirring as contents firm. Leave aside to cool.

Melon paste

In a blender or with a handheld mixer blend garlic cloves, ginger, capers and peeled melon. Blend everything until you have a smooth cream.

Fold in Korean chilli flakes into the melon paste and mix well.

Putting everything together

Slice the carrots into disks with a knife or a food processor.

Mix these carrot slices with the well-squeezed Chinese leaf. Then add the melon paste, and the rice flour cream which should have cooled down by now. Mix everything and massage with your hands. You may want to wear gloves for this as the chilli flakes may burn any cuts or wounds.

Fermentation

Put the contents in a container leaving a third of air space. Any container such as a large glass jar, a metal box or even a plastic bowl will do. Let it rest in a dry place for two days. You will notice that liquid will collect at the bottom and the top might remain dry. If so, it's important to mix the contents occasionally.

After 2 days, taste and gauge how well the fermentation has processed as this depends on the temperature in your house or environment. The taste should be slightly sour but not overwhelmingly so. This is not an exact science and depends on personal preference. You may extend fermentation for another day or two as the taste and texture can change quickly. Once you're happy with the fermentation stage, move the kimchi to the fridge. Be aware that it will continue to ferment there albeit much slower.

KIMCHI YELLOW

A crunchier version than the original with inflammation-fighting turmeric.

Ingredients

1,5kg (2) white radish (daikon/mooli)
100g (1) small fresh carrot
25g (1.5 tbsp) salt
10g (1 tbsp) capers
10g (3 tsp) garlic
10g (3 tsp) ginger roots
¼ honey melon
1g (½ tsp) turmeric powder
10g (3 tsp) rice powder
100ml (¼ cup + 3 tbsp) water

Preparation

Take the white radish, slice sidewise, cut it horizontally and then vertically to obtain small sticks no longer than 2cm (¾ inch) and no more 0.5cm (1/5 inch).

Put the cut white radish in a bowl, add salt and mix with your hands.

Leave to sit for 12 hours, then drain and press to remove all water.

Rice cream

Take a sauce pot and put rice flour and ambient water in it. Heat mixture on the hob and keep stirring as contents firm. Leave aside to cool.

Melon paste

This is the same as used for the Red Kimchi but uses turmeric instead of chilli flakes. In a blender or with a handheld mixer blend garlic cloves, ginger, capers turmeric and peeled melon. Blend everything until you have a smooth cream.

Putting everything together

Slice the carrots into disks with a knife or a food processor.

Mix the carrots with the well-pressed white radish, then add the rice cream, mix everything and massage the vegetables well to spread the cream evenly.

Place contents in a lidded jar and leave around a third of free space. Rest in a dry place for two days.

Until the kimchi is ready, you might notice that the liquid level recedes and the top of the vegetable mix might become dry. In that case give the mix a good stir every now and then

After 2 days, taste to check on the fermentation progress. This is not an exact science and it depends on your taste. It should taste tangy and slightly sour, a slight taste of vinegar. If too mild, let it ferment for another 1-2 days until the desired taste is achieved. When ready, store it in the fridge for up to several months.

KIMCHI GREEN

A mild refreshing mint taste and a healthy dose of spirulina, bursting with nutrients and antioxidants.

Ingredients

1.5kg (3 heads) white cabbage
25g (1.5 tbsp) salt
10g (2 tbsp) capers
10g (3 tsp) garlic
10g (3 tsp) ginger roots
¼ honey melon
3-5 twigs of fresh mint
½ tsp of spirulina powder
10g (3 tsp) rice powder
100ml (¼ cup + 3 tbsp) water

Preparation

Take the white cabbage and cut it with the knife into slices, then cut it horizontally and then vertically to obtain strips no longer than 2cm (3/4 inch).

Put the white cabbage in a bowl and add the salt. Mix with your hands.

Leave the white cabbage in salt for 12 hours, then drain and squeeze it to remove all the water.

Rice cream

Take a sauce pot and put rice flour and ambient water in it. Heat mixture on the hob and keep stirring as contents firm. Leave aside to cool.

Melon paste

In a blender or with a handheld mixer blend garlic cloves, ginger, capers, mint, spirulina and peeled melon. Blend everything until you have a smooth cream.

> Tip: Based on suggestion from a famous chef from Pisa, I recommend you use fresh mint including the stems as they are the most fragrant part of the plant.

Putting everything together

Combine the well squeezed white cabbage, with the cream and the cold rice flour, mix and massage everything in order to mix well.

Place contents in a lidded jar and leave around a third of free space. Rest in a dry place for two days.

Until the kimchi is ready, you might notice that the liquid level recedes and the top of the vegetable mix might become dry. In that case give the mix a good stir every now and then

After 2 days, taste to check on the fermentation progress. This is not an exact science and it depends on your taste. It should taste tangy and slightly sour, a slight taste of vinegar. If too mild, let it ferment for another 1-2 days until the desired taste is achieved. When ready, store it in the fridge for up to several months.

KIMCHI VIOLA

Intensely colourful, this purple variant is crunchy and mild.

보라

Viola

Ingredients

1.5kg (3 heads) red cabbage

25g (1.5 tbsp) salt

10g (2 tbsp) capers

10g (3 tsp) garlic

10g (3 tsp) ginger roots

¼ honey melon

1 tablespoon dried rosemary

10g (3 tsp) rice powder

100ml (¼ + 3 tbsp) water

Rosemary adds a distinctly Mediterranean touch and helps improve memory

Preparation

Take the red cabbage and cut it with the knife into slices, then cut it horizontally and then vertically to obtain strips no longer than 2cm (¾ inch). You might want to wear gloves as your fingers will become purple!

Put the red cabbage in a bowl and add the salt. Mix with your hands.

Leave the red cabbage in salt for 12 hours, then drain and squeeze it to remove all the water.

Rice cream

Take a sauce pot and put rice flour and ambient water in it. Heat mixture on the hob and keep stirring as contents firm. Leave aside to cool.

Melon paste

In a blender or with a handheld mixer blend garlic cloves, ginger, capers, dried rosemary and peeled melon. Blend everything until you have a smooth cream.

Putting everything together

Combine the well squeezed red cabbage, with the cream and the cold rice flour, mix and massage everything in order to mix well.

Place contents in a lidded jar and leave around a third of free space. Rest in a dry place for two days.

Until the kimchi is ready, you might notice that the liquid level recedes and the top of the vegetable mix might become dry. In that case give the mix a good stir every now and then

After 2 days, taste to check on the fermentation progress. This is not an exact science and it depends on your taste. It should taste tangy and slightly sour, a slight taste of vinegar. If too mild, let it ferment for another 1-2 days until the desired taste is achieved.

When ready, store it in the fridge for up to several months.

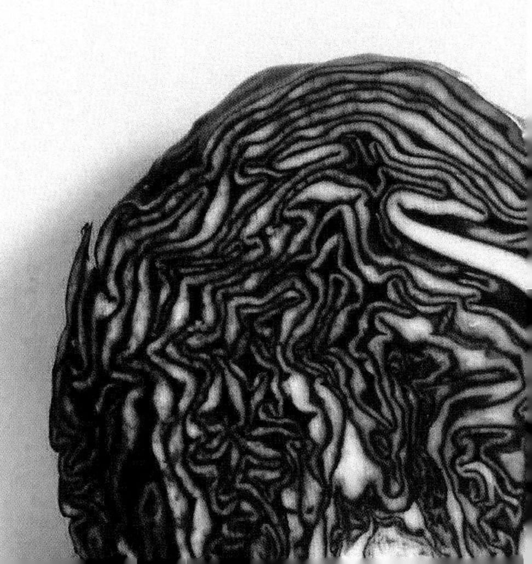

KIMCHI MAYONNAISE

Vegan mayo is incredibly easy to make and kimchi adds a tangy probiotic punch.

Ingredients

70g (½ cup) red, green/yellow or viola kimchi

20g (1 ½ tbsp) apple vinegar, lemon juice or lime juice

5g (½ tsp) salt

100g (½ cup) extra virgin olive oil

200g (1 cup) organic cold pressed sunflower oil

100g (½ cup) of soya milk

> We use mostly sunflower oil as olive oil is heavy and imparts a particular taste

Preparation

Put the kimchi in a bowl, add salt, vinegar/lemon/lime and then the oils and soya milk. With a handheld blender, blend the ingredients well by moving up and down and then in circular motions. Stays fresh for 3 days in the fridge.

KIMCHI TOAST

A very quick and simple dish or those extra busy days!

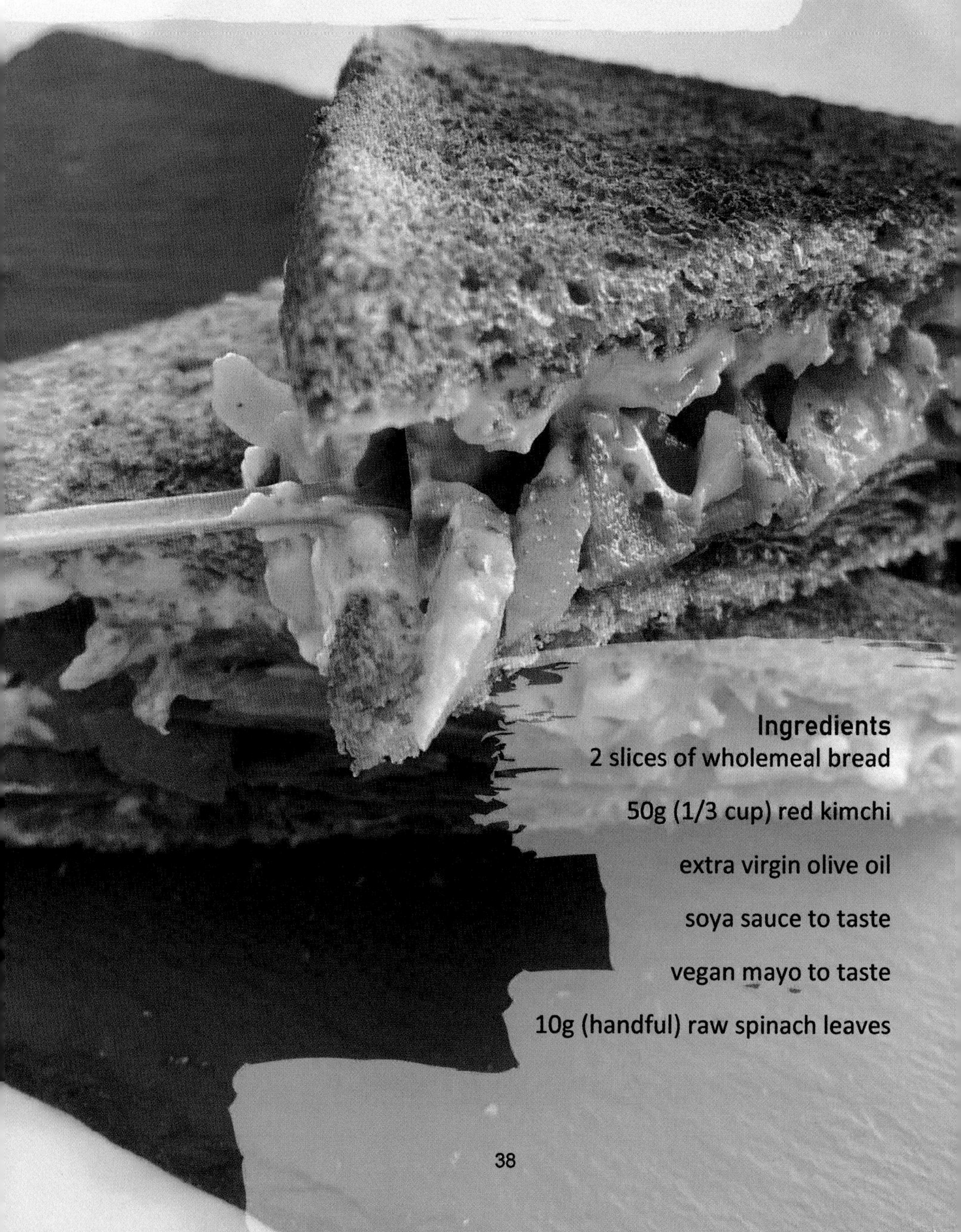

Ingredients

2 slices of wholemeal bread

50g (1/3 cup) red kimchi

extra virgin olive oil

soya sauce to taste

vegan mayo to taste

10g (handful) raw spinach leaves

Preparation

Toast the bread then spread some mayonnaise on both slices. Place spinach onto one slice, add a generous amount of red kimchi and then season with soya sauce and extra virgin olive oil. Cover with the other slice of bread, cut the toast in half diagonally and serve on the plate.

KIMCHI HUMMUS

Ingredients

- 240g (1 can) of drained chickpeas
- 240g (1 ½ cups) of red kimchi
- Juice of half a lemon
- 2 cloves of fresh garlic
- 50g (½ cup) extra virgin olive oil

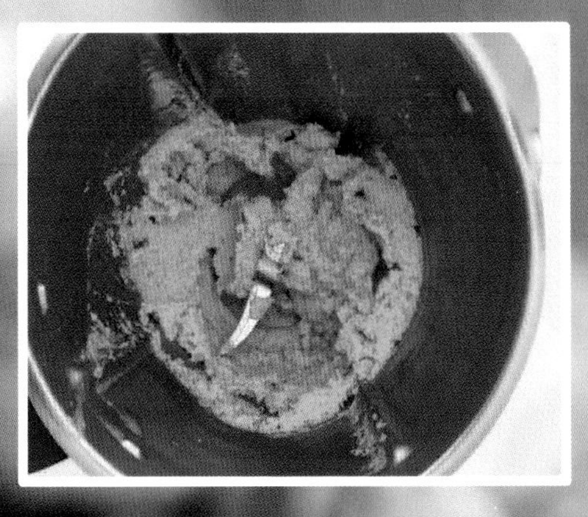

Preparation

Put kimchi in a blender, add garlic, chickpeas, lemon juice and oil, whisk everything until desired consistency is achieved. Some like it chunky, some smooth.

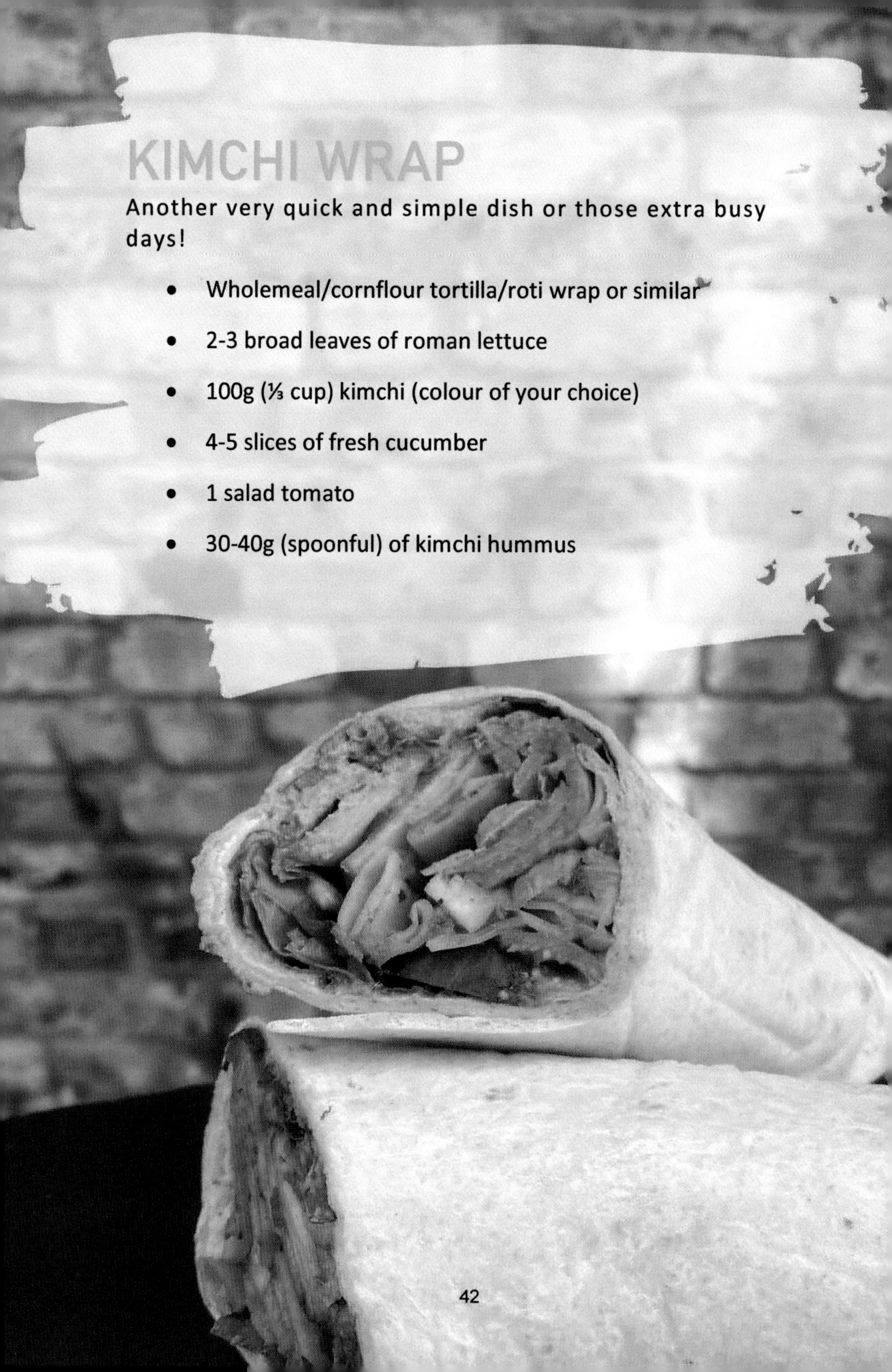

KIMCHI WRAP

Another very quick and simple dish or those extra busy days!

- Wholemeal/cornflour tortilla/roti wrap or similar
- 2-3 broad leaves of roman lettuce
- 100g (⅓ cup) kimchi (colour of your choice)
- 4-5 slices of fresh cucumber
- 1 salad tomato
- 30-40g (spoonful) of kimchi hummus

Preparation

Take the wrap and spread it with kimchi hummus, add all other ingredients, fold it like a burrito and place it on a baking sheet, heat it in the oven at 250 ° for 3-5 minutes.

STEAMED RICE

A staple food all over the world including Korea. It's quick and easy when you do it correctly.

Ingredients

200g (¾ cup) of rice

230g (1 ¼ cup) of water

Preparation

Put the rice and water in a saucepan, cover with lid and leave on high heat until the lid begins to move. At that point lower the flame to the minimum and let it cook for 8-10 more minutes. I personally also judge the rice to be ready when I peak through the glass lid and see little holes forming as seen in the picture. Once done, let rest for 1 minute and then fluff up with a fork.

KIMCHI INARI

This dish is too easy to prepare but excellent as an appetizer or aperitif.

Ingredients

Inari pocket (Made with deep-fried sweetened tofu, known as abura-age in Japanese and found in East Asian supermarkets)

Kimchi (colour of your choice)

Boiled rice

5g Extra virgin olive oil

5g Soya sauce

1g (½ tsp) Black or white sesame seeds

Preparation

Open the tofu pocket and fill it with boiled rice. Wet a finger and poke a hole in the centre of the rice inside and fill it with a colour of kimchi of your choice. Season with soya sauce first and extra virgin olive oil after. Sprinkle some white or black sesame seeds to highlight the colour of the kimchi you have chosen. Serve immediately as the rice dries quickly.

KIMCHI KIMBAP

Kimbap is what the sushi roll is called in Korean, it seems difficult but it is as simple as rolling a newspaper.

Made with either red, yellow, green or purple kimchi, this is a perfect lunch box filler or served as a side. 2-3 rolls make a full meal that you could serve with some dressed spinach on the side.

To mix things up, you could also fill the roll with other vegetables such as cucumber, carrot sticks, sweet potato, tofu, turnip tops, avocado, sundried tomatoes, green beans, mayo...

I even make chocolate kimbap! Crazy, I know. If you want to try this, wait for the rice to completely cool before adding the chocolate squares.

Ingredients

- Steamed rice (see steamed rice recipe)
- Bamboo mat
- Nori seaweed sheets for sushi
- Kimchi
- Sesame seeds
- Extra virgin olive oil
- Soya sauce

Preparation

Place the bamboo mat horizontally in front of you on the table, place the nori sheet on top.

Put the rice on the seaweed making a layer 1- 2 centimetres high (0.5 inch), leave 2cm (¾ inch) of empty space on one end of the nori sheet closest to you and as many 2- 3 centimetres (1 inch) space on the opposite end.

Form a strip of layered kimchi horizontally in the centre of the rice, and now 'roll up the newspaper'!

The trick is that the part of the nori sheet closest to you will stick on the opposing end of the sheet without rice on it. Roll up the whole wrap and then roll slightly back take away the bamboo roll and let the nori sheet ends stick together. Seal the seam of your roll by brushing and lightly pressing it with a wet finger to make it really glue together. This is the trickiest part and hence you can find a YouTube video on it on my "Vegan Yes" channel!

Note that the nori sheet needs to be aligned to the very end of the bamboo mat from where you start rolling.

After you formed your roll, move it onto a chopping board, use a well-sharpened knife or e, the knife works well if it is wet and free from rice, so wash it and leave it wet even between cuts. Arrange the kimbap pieces on a plate, season with soya sauce and extra virgin olive oil, put some more of the kimchi you used earlier on top and add soya sauce and extra virgin olive oil, garnish with sesame seeds and the dish is ready.

KIMCHI BIBIMBAP

Bibimbap is of synonymous of Korea as Lasagna is to Italy or the Hamburger to America. The name identifies both the main ingredient and the method in which to eat it, *Bap* in Korean means Rice and *Bibim* means *mixing*. The name of this dish is mixed rice.

The base of this dish is a steamed rice ball that is placed in the centre of the dish, the rest is up to the chef's imagination... that's you! Go crazy in creating your BIBIMBAP!

My creation is what you find here. Presenting the KIMCHI BIBIMBAP!

Ingredients

50g (1 cup) red kimchi

50g (1 cup) green kimchi

50g (1 cup) yellow kimchi

50g (1 cup) purple kimchi

200g (heaped bowl) boiled rice (see below)

50g (Handful) of fresh spinach

Dressing: a sprinkle black or white sesame seeds, spring onions (scallion), extra virgin olive oil, soya sauce

Preparation

Cut the spring onion 2-3 millimetres (0.2 inch), put it in a container with cold water to rest for at least 1 hour. Like that it becomes more digestible while maintaining its freshness.

Once the rice has finished cooking, prepare assembly of the dish: get a small bowl that will serve as a mould for the rice dome, fill the rice bowl with the help of a spatula, turn the bowl upside down and put it in the centre of the plate.

Now place the spinach around the rice filling the whole plate. Next put the four colours of kimchi over the spinach. I personally like to balance the colours: The light colours (red and yellow) facing each other and sprinkled with black sesame seeds and the darker colours (green and purple) sprinkled with white sesame seeds.

Before you sprinkle the sesame seeds on top, season with soya sauce first and next extra oil virgin olive oil. Lastly, take the spring onions from their soak bath and put them in the centre on top of the rice.

KIMCHI LASAGNA

History

My Kimchi lasagna invention is based on a memory from my childhood. When I was a child, I saw *la nonna* (grandmother) Maria preparing fresh pasta sheets by hand. She started by simply mixing flour and water, forming a ball of dough and then spread it with a rolling pin, slowly spreading it to grow larger and larger, up to the size of the whole table!

One strong lasting memory is that of the fabulous colours of the pasta sheets: Sunshine yellow (made with egg) or even with spinach). Those colours still come back in their vibrancy in front of my eyes after all those years!

After this, *la nonna* cooked these huge sheets in boiling water and then put them in a pan and spread béchamel and Bolognese sauce and finally covered everything with Parmesan.

Finally, the masterpiece would be completed. Eating this lasagna created an explosion of flavours in one's mouth: The soft homemade pasta caressing the tongue, combining with the rich melt-in-mouth bechamel sauce.

With these everlasting memories etched into my life, you can understand that the union of lasagna and kimchi was obvious to me. The love I feel for my wife is enormous and her attachment to her tradition has infected me alike, after many years of living together and the countless times that I have been able to experience and taste East Asian culture on trips made with her. One day, I decided to ensure that this joy and harmony that united us and made us so strong should be translated onto the plate and that everyone could savour and relive that feeling that I feel for my wife.

The fusion of two worlds Korea and Italy, East and West, two parts so distant and so different from our planet that putting them together seems almost impossible but instead life has taught me that everything is possible, you just have to wish for it.

So below you can find the recipe to prepare this wonderful invention, born out of passion and love.

Lasagna pasta sheets

It's of course possible to buy ready-made sheets (including gluten-free options) but here is my recipe to make it from scratch:

Ingredients

- 250g (2 cups) ground semolina
- 250g (2 cups) Type "00" wheat flour
- 2g (½ tsp) ground turmeric
- 250g (1 cup) water

Preparation

Mix the semolina with the flour and make a mountain on a chopping board or in a bowl, make a small space in the centre, pour a little water and mix with the turmeric.

With your fingertips, start kneading, slowly incorporating the flour towards the centre. Add the water little by little, continuing to knead until a smooth, soft but not sticky dough is obtained.

Put the dough in a container, cover it with plastic wrap and let it rest out of the fridge for about thirty minutes.

After the rest time you can take your dough and begin to work it with a rolling pin to create fine dough sheets for your lasagna, if you have the machine to roll out the dough the thickness measurement is 2 or 3mm (0.11 inch).

Once you have created your sheets, put them in a tray and between them spread some semolina so that they do not stick together.

Bechamel sauce for Lasagna

Ingredients

- 75g (½ cup + 1 tbsp) extra virgin olive oil
- 150g (1 ½ cups) Type "00" flour
- 5g (1 tsp) of ground pepper
- 5g (1 tsp) of ground nutmeg
- 1.5l (6 cups) soya milk or vegetable broth
- 15g (3 tsp) of salt

Procedure

Put oil in a pot, slowly pour in the flour whilst turning with a whisk. Add the milk or broth and spices, put the pot on the stove over medium heat and continue to stir with the whisk until the bechamel begins to form bubbles, remove from heat and set aside.

Lasagna filling

Ingredients

2.5kg (3 heads) Chinese leaf (Napa cabbage)

100g (5 oz) Korean chilli flakes

Preparation

Cut the Chinese cabbage into 4 parts, after which cut it into thin strips, half the size of what you did for the red kimchi, put it in a large container, add the chili pepper and mix well with your hands. Make sure to mix the chilli well and massage it into the cabbage chunks, turning its colour red like fire! Set aside.

VEGAN PARMESAN

Ingredients

150g (1 cup) whole or shelled hemp seeds

300g (3 cups) whole or ground almonds

200g (2 cups) sunflower seeds

50g (½ cup) sesame seeds

10g (1 tsp) black salt
(sold in South Asian supermarkets as *kala namak*)

50g (½ cup) of nutritional yeast flakes

Yields 760g/7 cups. Nutrition per 2 tbsp (20g) serving: 111 calories, 9g fat, 5g protein, 5g carbohydrates (of which 1g sugar).

Preparation

Blend all ingredients apart from the nutritional yeast in a blender. If you have a less powerful one or only a spice blender, blend the ingredients in batches.

At the end transfer to a bowl and add the yeast flakes. Mix with a spatula from the bottom upwards gently, so that the pieces of yeast remain as intact as possible.

Lasagna preparation

We have a YouTube video on the assembly

Now that all the elements are ready, let's get a nice high lasagna tray and start the composition.

Spread the béchamel on the bottom of the tray with a spoon. Now spread the pasta sheets without leaving any empty spaces and without overlapping.

Cover the pasta with a layer of bechamel, spread it with a spoon being careful not to move the sheets below.

Now place a generous layer of chilled cabbage followed by a nice spread of red kimchi (include any kimchi brine you have so it flows into the cabbage layer).

Press down lightly with your hands.

Now layer some more pasta sheets and cover it with béchamel sauce, add chilled cabbage and red kimchi and again some of its brine if you have.

Repeat these steps until the tray is full, finishing with pasta sheets generously covered with bechamel.

Then sprinkle the vegan parmesan on top and bake at 180°C (350° F) for 45-60 minutes.

Once fully baked, wait for it to cool a bit before cutting it. Serve with a side salad (I like just spinach sometimes) seasoned with soya sauce, extra virgin olive oil and vegan parmesan.

KIMCHI CAPRESE

Caprese is a typical Italian side dish consisting of sliced mozzarella, tomatoes and fresh basil.

Kimchi Caprese found its birth in a moment of huge disappointment in my life. I was in London in the summer of 2016 where I toured all the most imported markets for the in search of the best tomatoes. I bought and tasted all kinds of varieties offered until I finally resigned in the recognition that London tomatoes may be named the same, may be as red and look like Italian tomatoes... but the taste definitely is not! Not even close to the pleasure real sundrenched Italian tomatoes can impart.

Whatever the reason for this lack of taste of these imported goods, I decided I had to replace tomatoes with kimchi in my version of caprese. At last I got my smile back!

Vegan Mozzarella

Our mozzarella classes taught in 2018 in our restaurant on Brick Lane have been hugely popular. There was an explosion of interest in veganism that year specifically so many people were intrigued in learning about vegan cooking. A lot of vegan-curious people told us that cheese is what they'd miss the most so this recipe was one of the most requested. Most vegan cheeses use soaked nuts but this one can be made without any preparation! There is a video of how to prepare this mozzarella on our YouTube page if you prefer to see how it works!

Ingredients

- 60g (½ cup) extra virgin olive oil
- 60g (½ cup) soya milk
- Another 180g (1 ½ cups) soya milk
- 200g (1 cup) coconut yogurt
- 150g (1 cup) potato starch
- 5g (1 tsp) salt
- 2g (1 tsp) dried rosemary

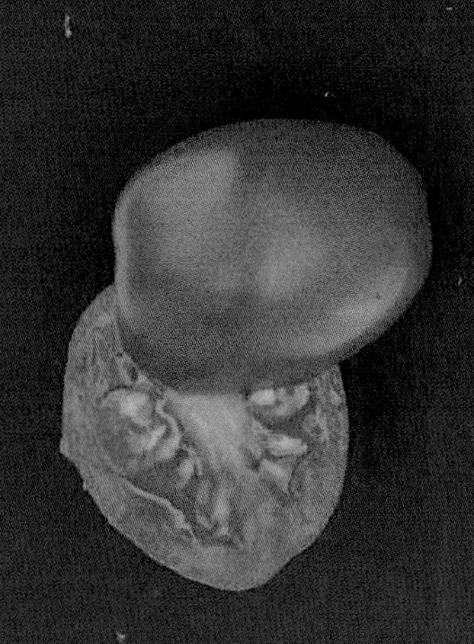

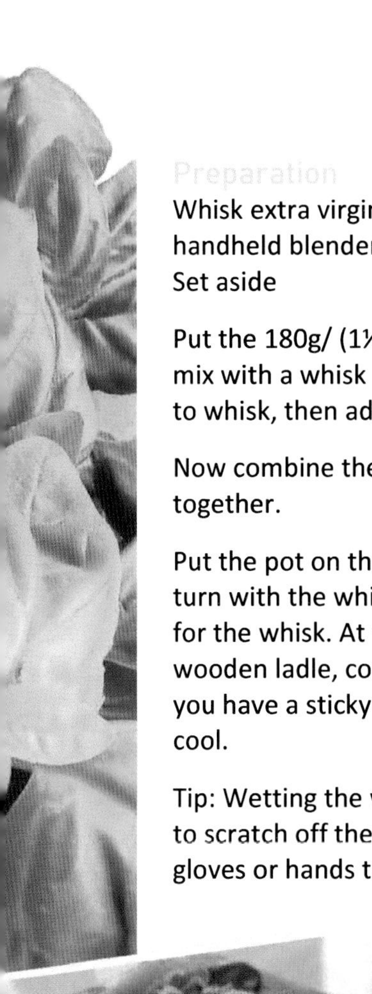

Preparation

Whisk extra virgin olive oils and 60g/ (½ cup) soya milk with a handheld blender. The mixture should increase in volume. Set aside

Put the 180g/ (1½ cups) of soya milk and yogurt in a steel pot, mix with a whisk and slowly add the potato starch. Continue to whisk, then add the salt and rosemary.

Now combine the two mixtures and continue to whisk together.

Put the pot on the stove over medium heat and continue to turn with the whisk until the contents have become too thick for the whisk. At this point lower the heat and move to a wooden ladle, continue to turn by hand. Keep turning until you have a sticky ball, then remove the pot from the heat and cool.

Tip: Wetting the wooden ladle with cold water will help you to scratch off the mozzarella dough from the pot. Use a wet gloves or hands to form any shape you want. Traditionally it's an oval ball shape.

Place in a dish for or wrap in cling film.

Put it in the fridge for at least 12 hours, after which it will have hardened and is ready to eat.

If you leave the mozzarella in the fridge for a few more days you will notice that the consistency changes gradually and it becomes harder. From the third or fourth day, it can be crumbled with your hands onto pizza for example or baked like halloumi cheese.

CAPRESE

This aromatic and healthy side dish is popular in summer and referred to as "*tricolore*" because its colours resemble the Italian flag: Red, white and green!

Ingredients

- mozzarella cheese
- red kimchi
- basil
- extra virgin olive oil
- ground pepper
- soya sauce

Preparation

Lay one slice of mozzarella, then some kimchi and repeat.

Sprinkle with fresh basil, some soya sauce and extra virgin olive oil. Then grind some black pepper onto the sliced mozzarella.

KIMCHI AND FASULE

This dish is rich in protein thanks to the black beans. To call this simple combination a dish is almost presumptuous but I nevertheless dedicated it to my Neapolitan father where beans are called FASULE. The recipe remained in the drawer for a few years until I decided to put it on the restaurant's menu and people appreciated the name and taste!

Ingredients

- 200g (7.1 oz) dried black beans or one can (called *frijoles negros* in Latin markets)
- 2 cloves of garlic
- Black and white sesame
- Extra virgin olive oil
- Soya sauce
- Steamed rice

Preparation

Soak the beans in water for one night. The next day, drain them, rinse with fresh water, put in a pan with the two cloves of garlic, and little water and two table spoons of soya sauce. Cover the and cook over low heat for 45 minutes. (Alternatively buy canned beans rinse with water and heat in a pot with the two cloves of garlic).

Spread cooked rice diagonally onto a plate, put beans on one side and kimchi on the other side. Season with soya sauce, extra virgin olive oil and sprinkle with white and black sesame seeds.

LA PIRAMIDE

Another very simple dish to prepare and that's precisely why it was born. One day, an employee of mine pointed out that we should have an item that we could promote as "From menu to belly in two minutes". This simple but now very popular item was born: One type of Kimchi piled onto rice, piled onto Spinach. We called it "the pyramid" for its form that is towering to heaven.

Ingredients

- 50g (2 handful) of baby spinach
- 150g (1 bowl) of steamed rice
- 5g (½ cup) dry seaweed (*wakame*)
- 80g (1 cup) Kimchi Viola
- Seasoning: 15g/1tbsp Extra virgin olive oil, 15g/1tbsp Soya sauce, 20g/2tbsp vegan parmesan, 5g/1tsp sesame seeds

Nutrition: 504 calories, 27g fat, 13g protein, 54g carbs of which 4g sugar.

Preparation

Put the dried seaweed in a bowl with water. Cold water will suffice as you will need time to prepare the rest. Use boiled water if in a rush and your tummy is growling.

Boil rice and place it in a small bowl. Place the bowl upside down onto a flat plate. Press with spatula to flatten, take the seaweed and squeeze with hand, cut with scissors and assemble on top the rice. Spread spinach around the rice, put the kimchi on top of the seaweed and try to fluff up the top to form a pyramid.

Season with extra virgin olive oil, soya sauce. Then spread vegan parmesan on top the spinach and sesame seeds on top the kimchi. Buon appetite!

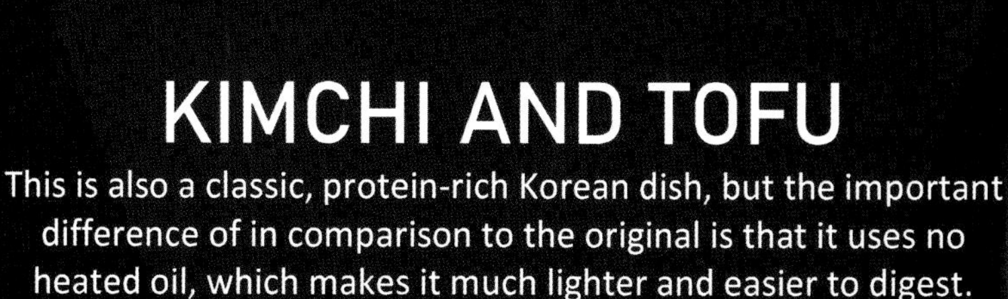

KIMCHI AND TOFU

This is also a classic, protein-rich Korean dish, but the important difference of in comparison to the original is that it uses no heated oil, which makes it much lighter and easier to digest.

Ingredients

1 block of fresh tofu

Extra virgin olive oil

Soya sauce

Black sesame seeds

Steamed rice

Chives

Kimchi

Preparation

Cut the tofu block into strips no more than 1cm thick, arrange the slices in a non-stick pan and put on medium heat. Once it started browning on one side, remove the pan from the heat. You now have 2 options:

1) Cover pan with a lid for 10 minutes, after which you will notice drops of condensation forming. Perform a dance or sing in the meantime. After that, turn your tofu sliced for the next step.

2) Immediately pour some cold water which will "thermally shock" the tofu and allow it from being peeled from the pan with ease.

Now with the second, uncooked side facing down, turn heat to medium until the other side of tofu is roasted. At this point you can insert the red kimchi with some of its liquid, cover and let it cook for 2 minutes. Turn off the heat and wait a minute before lifting the lid to serve You will see that the tofu will come off the pan easily.

Serve with a portion of steamed rice, season with soya sauce and extra virgin olive oil, garnish with black sesame seeds and chives.

YELLOW BREAD

My basis for an accompaniment to many dishes including the recipe for Bruschetta that follows. The bread is yellow from the turmeric, which is an anti-inflammatory Ayurvedic superfood.

Ingredients

500g (5 cups) Type "00" flour

500g (5 cups) whole wheat flour

500ml (2 cups) water

50g (⅓ cup) sunflower seeds

20g (2 tbsp) black sesame seeds

10g (2 tbsp) Korean chilli flakes

30g (5 tsp) salt

5g (1 tsp) ground turmeric powder

8g (1 tsp) dry yeast (usually one sachet)

Preparation

Pour the flour, turmeric, chilli pepper, sunflower seeds and black sesame seeds into a wide mixing bowl.

Dissolve the salt in 100g / (½ cup) of water, and mix it with the flour, mixing everything.

Put the yeast in a container and pour 400g / (1 ½ cups) of lukewarm water, turn to dissolve the yeast after which add it to the flour and knead.

Once a consistent dough is obtained, wrap it in plastic wrap and let it rest for 24 hours.

After 24 hours, take the dough, remove it from the foil and fold it over again for at least 5/10 minutes.

Finally, shape the bread and place onto a baking pan and let it rest for at least 8 hours.

Bake at 220 ° for 40-50 minutes.

KIMCHI BRUSCHETTA

Koreas main stable food is rice whereas in Italy, we eat a lot of bread. The traditional Italian starter or snack called bruschetta is composed of a slice of bread (see recipe) often roasted with extra virgin olive oil and something else, for example, garlic, cherry tomatoes, beans, mushrooms. I did it with kimchi.

Ingredients

- sliced bread
- red / yellow / green / purple kimchi
- fresh garlic
- extra virgin olive oil
- soya sauce
- vegan parmesan

Preparation

Take the slices of bread and roast them in the oven / toaster. Rub the top of the toast with a glove of garlic. Put the slice on the plate and cover it with kimchi colour of your choice, season with soya sauce, extra virgin olive oil and vegan parmesan.

KIMCHI & WATERMELON

This recipe derives from a true story. My wife was considered a bit naughty when she was child. For that reason, her mother always held her by the hand in order to keep her in her line of sight. One day, her mother went to the local Buddhist temple as she would every now and then. Little Min was playing outside the temple and was attracted by a watermelon plantation. She approached the nearest watermelon and began knocking on it. The knock's sound echoeing inside the watermelon intrigued her. Curiously, she took a hammer and started banging on the watermelon. The echo inside became even more apparent but it all culminated in a bang when the watermelon finally broke. "Wow!", "Again!". Little Min moved onto the next watermelon to experience the sounds again. But like with a musical instrument that can only be played once, she moved from one watermelon to the next on the plantation.

But when the farmer arrived, the concert was over. The man exasperatedly asked her what she had done!

Innocently, little Min replied that she liked the music.

The very angry farmer said to her:

- So you like music?

- Then you shall sing until sunset!

The farmer whipped out a bamboo cane and every time she stopped singing, she was poked with the cane to remind her to continue.

At sunset the mother and the monks of the temple came looking for her and saw the disaster.

Once the farmer reported what brought this about, she agreed to buy all the broken watermelons and donated them to the temple.

The monks at the temple devoured the watermelon slices in delight and prepared a dish with the leftover white part of the slices, cooking it with soya sauce, garlic and sesame oil.

We will now share our updated version of this old recipe with you, which ingeniously uses the leftover white part of the watermelon that is usually discarded.

Ingredients

- White part of the watermelon, peeled. Weigh it as the rest of the recipe depends on how much you have.
- soya sauce, 1% of the weight of the watermelon bits
- garlic, 2% of the weight of the watermelon bits
- Same amount of kimchi as watermelon
- Extra virgin olive oil for seasoning
- White sesame for garnishing

Preparation

Chop the garlic and mix with the chopped watermelon bits in a container with soya sauce, leave to rest for a few hours.

Cook in a pan with a lid for 20 minutes over medium heat.

Remove some of the liquid that has formed and stir-fry with the red kimchi for 5 minutes over medium heat.

Serve and season with extra virgin olive oil and garnish with sesame seeds.

Serve as a side dish or accompanied with steamed rice.

POMODORO

Tomato sauce, "Pomodoro" is another hallmark of Italian culture. My grandmother, my aunts, relatives and friends all made their own version of it. La Nona Antonietta, my dad's mum made a potful every week. Stored in the fridge, she helped herself to it whenever a recipe called for a tomato sauce base. My take on tomato sauce is made without heated oil, making it lighter and healthier.

Ingredients

250g (3) carrots

100g (2) white onions

½ cube of vegetable stock

10g (½ tbsp) salt

4 cans (400g) of peeled (not chopped) tomatoes

Preparation

Blend carrots and onions in a blender to create a creamy mixture. Transfer to a large pot, heat over medium heat and cover with lid. Stir occasionally and cook until carrots become lighter in colour and shinier. In the meantime, open a can of peeled tomatoes and blend in food processor. Add tomatoes to carrot onion mixture, rinse the can and add a third of the jar of water to your sauce. Next, add the salt and vegetable stock. Lower heat and continue cooking for at least 4 hours, turning occasionally with the lid on in between. Only lift the lid slightly in the last hour

KIMCHI PARMIGIANA

Parmesan is a traditional Italian dish and my grandmother Antonietta, being from the South, knew how to make it herself!

I remember the smell of fried aubergine (eggplant) soaking in oil drying on paper towels, the frying pan of tomato sauce still sizzling on the fire, slowly boiling away since the morning. The final touch of the recipe was the mozzarella that my father brought her freshly from Naples.

Today I present to you an oil-free, cholesterol-free and unsaturated fat-free recipe, with a hint of spice imparted from the red kimchi used here.

Ingredients

4 Aubergines

Coarse sea salt to taste

Vegan Mozzarella to taste

500g (2 cups) tomato sauce

Vegan Parmesan to taste

200g (4 cups) Red Kimchi

Preparation

Cut the aubergines into 1cm (0.5 inch) thick slices, arrange them on a tray and sprinkle them with salt. Tilt the tray to let the water released by the vegetable flow out. This ensures that the aubergines won't be bitter.

After a few hours the aubergines will have released all its water. Dry them with a paper towel and arrange on an oven tray. Bake at 180-200°C (350-400°F) until they are well roasted but not too dry.

At this point, take the baking tray and spread some of the tomato sauce and replace the aubergine slices.

Spread 100g (2 cups) of red kimchi on top of the aubergines and then cover with more tomato sauce, now add the crumbled mozzarella with your hands or cut it into small pieces.

Now make another layer of aubergines, pressing a little to compact everything, add the remaining 100g (2 cups) of red kimchi on top of the aubergines, then plenty of tomato sauce and mozzarella. Make sure that the mozzarella is well mixed with the tomato sauce. Sprinkle everything with plenty of vegan parmesan.

Bake 180°C (350°F) for 45 minutes, leave to cool before cutting and serve.

RAW KIMCHI SEASONED

PECORINO

A term for Italian hard cheese, although originally referring to a particular kind from Sardinia made from sheep's milk. My version is made with nuts and maca powder, which imparts a particular taste whilst at the same time bursting with hormone-boosting health benefits.

Ingredients

- 140g (1 cup) Macadamia nuts
- 140g (1 cup) Cashews nuts
- 60g (¼ cup) water
- 1 capsule of vegan probiotics
- 5g (1 tsp) Maca powder
- 10g (2 tbsp) coconut oil
- 10g (2 tbsp) lemon juice
- 1 pinch of salt
- 1g (½ tsp) of dried garlic powder
- 50g (1 cup) of red kimchi
- 5g (1 tbsp) of Korean chilli flakes

Preparation

Soak the macadamia nuts and cashews for at least 12 hours. Then rinse them well, drain and add to 60g/ (¼ cup) of water. Take out the powder of a probiotic capsule and add everything in a mixer.

Blend everything until obtaining a smooth, lump-free cream and insert the mixture in two ricotta mould baskets to let out any liquid, put the moulds in a dish covered with a cloth and place them in a dry and dark place for 48 hours.

After two days, remove the mixture from the mould and put it in the mixer, adding 5g/ (1 tsp) of maca powder, 10g/(2tsp) of lemon juice and a pinch of salt. Whisk everything, then wrap airtight in plastic cling film. Place in the refrigerator for 24 hours to continue its fermentation.

Take 50g/ (1 cup) of kimchi, squeeze to remove excess liquid and put in a dehydrator for 12 hours at 45 degrees (150 Fahrenheit). There is a way to do this in a conventional oven but you may have to research this.

After 24 hours, take the nut mixture in the ricotta mould from the fridge, put it in a bowl and mix it with the dehydrated kimchi and the Korean chilli flakes. We will now use the ricotta mould to shape the mixture. Line it with baking paper (wet the paper and press it into the mould). Add the cheese mixture, then turn the mould upside down onto a tray. Remove the mould and peel off the baking paper. You now have the shaped mixture on a tray which you can place into the dehydrator again. Leave it at a temperature not exceeding 45 degrees (150 Fahrenheit) for at least 24 hours.

After 24 hours in the dehydrator, tightly wrap the two cheese blocks in baking paper and place inside an airtight, dated container.

Keep in the refrigerator to age for at least 30 days and up to several months.

KIMCHI PIE

This dish is my interpretation of the very popular "sformato" in Italy. My mom specialised in the "ricotta and spinach" version, a classic of Italian cuisine. Italian pies appear at family functions, parties, open air picnics and on special days as a meal that is easy to transport and can even be eaten cold.

My version of course uses kimchi and other vegetables as a filling! You could use any vegetables for your filling with kimchi, depending on what you have at home. Experiment and make it your own.

Ingredients

Base
- 1 pack ready rolled puff pastry
- Extra virgin olive oil for glazing

Filling
- 100g (2cups) Kimchi Red
- Vegetables of any kind, I used: 2 celery ribs, 1 carrot, 1 medium tomato, Curly kale 40g (1 cup), ½ onion

Protein
- 60g (¼ cup) of dry soya mince

Seasoning
- 4 cloves of garlic
- 1 tsp ginger powder

Seeds & Nuts
- 20g (2 tbsp) sunflower seeds
- 40g (8 tbsp) hazelnuts
- 40g (4 tbsp) almonds
- Sesame seeds
- 20g (4 tbsp) cocoa beans (their aftertaste reminds me of blue cheese!)

Preparation

Put the dry soya mince in a bowl with soy sauce and water, leave to hydrate.

Cut vegetables (celery, carrots, tomato, onion) into small pieces, place in a pot and add seasoning (ginger powder, chopped garlic, crushed cocoa beans).

Cook for 5 minutes then add the soya mince which should be fully rehydrated by now.

Cook for 10 minutes, stirring frequently until the mixture has reduced in size. Leave aside to cool and add your chopped nuts and seeds.

Take a large pie dish (20cm / 8 inch diameter) and line it with puff pastry. Cut off the edges and reserve strips to close it later.

Pour in your cooked mixture and press to distribute it neatly inside your form.

Take kimchi, squeeze out any excess liquid and place on top. Then gently press to compact everything.

Close your pie by taken your leftover strips of puff pastry and lining them up one atop each other in a checked pattern.

Brush the top with extra virgin olive oil and then sprinkle with sesame seeds.

Bake at 180 ° / (350 ° F) for 45 minutes.

Leave to cool before cutting into slices.

KIMCHI COCKTAILS

Although many friends and even my daughter Miso are passionate cocktail lovers, I never was attracted to mixology until I met Claudio. He is a young Italian guy, medium height, dark hair that now found himself in a foreign country working for a famous London hotel as a bartender. Our paths and passions crossed and he helped me invent my range of Kimchi cocktails.

As a dedication to my beloved ancestral home, the first Cocktail created by us was the Kimchi Negroni. The original Negroni was invented in Florence in 1919 by Count Camillo Negroni who used to frequent a bar now called Caffè Giacosa to drink a cocktail named Americano which included Campari, Vermouth and soda water. One fine day, Count Negroni returned from a trip to London with gin as a souvenir in his suitcase and asked the barman at Caffe Giacosa to add gin instead of soda water to his cocktail. Later, this new mix was named after the Count himself. In 2019, we celebrated the centenary of the Negroni cocktail and as a twist, we offer you the Kimchi Negroni.

KIMCHI NEGRONI

2.5 cl / (1 oz) Gin
2.5 cl / (1 oz) Martini Bianco
1 cl / (¼ oz) Velvet Falernum
1 cl / (¼ oz) Aperitif 30/40 de Normandie
1.5 cl / (½ oz) Purple Kimchi Juice
A lemon/orange
Ice

Pour in all liquids into a cocktail shaker with ice, stir slowly holding it until your hand is almost frozen. Use a strainer and pour contents into an old-fashioned glass to serve with one cube of ice. Zest your lemon on top and add a slice of the skin if you want.

KIMCHI MARGARITA

5 cl / (1 ¾ oz) tequila
3 cl / (1 ¼ oz) lemon juice
1.5 cl / (½ oz) agave syrup
1 cl / (½ oz) red Kimchi juice
Lemon peel
Salt
Ice

Place a slice of lemon into old-fashioned glass, wet half the edge of the glass, turn it upside down and place it on the salt so that it sticks to the rim.

Fill the glass with ice cubes as well as into half of your shaker. Pour all other ingredients into the shaker then close and shake for ten seconds. Pour the contents into the glass with the help of a strainer to hold back the cubes in the shaker. Squeeze the lemon peel over the cocktail to release some lemon oil scent onto it and then place the peel itself inside the glass to decorate

KIMCHI MOJITO

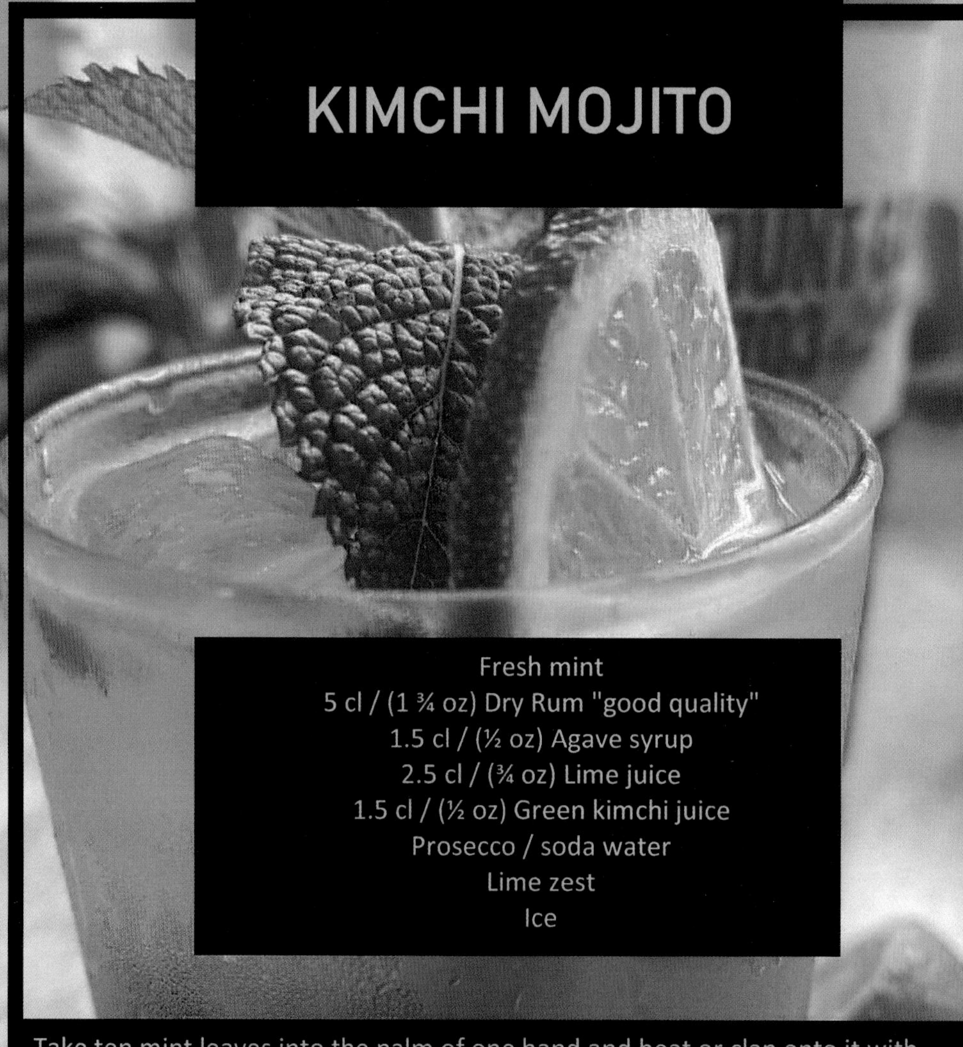

Fresh mint
5 cl / (1 ¾ oz) Dry Rum "good quality"
1.5 cl / (½ oz) Agave syrup
2.5 cl / (¾ oz) Lime juice
1.5 cl / (½ oz) Green kimchi juice
Prosecco / soda water
Lime zest
Ice

Take ten mint leaves into the palm of one hand and beat or clap onto it with your other balm to release the flavour.

Insert the leaves in a narrow, tall glass, add the ice cubes up to three quarters of the glass, then pour in the agave syrup, lime juice, rum and kimchi juice.

Take an ice cube in your hand and with the back of a hit the centre of the cube to break and crush it into small pieces. Then fill the glass with the crushed ice. Add prosecco or soda to the top. Add two sprigs of mint inserted into the glass and finish everything with a twist with the lime zest, add a straw and serve.

KIMCHI GUT LIVER

4 cl / (1 ½ oz) Whiskey
1.5 cl / (½ oz) Mescal
1.5 cl / (¼ oz) Vanilla syrup
1.5 cl / (¼ oz) Lemon juice
1.5 cl / (¼ oz) Yellow kimchi juice
Lemon peel
Ginger Kombucha
Ice

Prepare a shaker with two ice cubes, insert whiskey, mescal, vanilla syrup, lemon juice and yellow kimchi juice. Stir for ten seconds and pour into a tall glass full of ice. Top up with ginger kombucha, make a lemon twist and insert the peel inside the glass. Insert a straw and serve.

ACKNOWLEDGMENTS

First and foremost, my best friend and wife Min, who was brave enough to believe in my crazy ideas and support me on this magnificent journey, who shared emotions and joys with me, who supported me in every step I took.

I'm also indebted to my daughters, Cele, Miso and Iurì, for forgiving the absence from our homeland and sharing our love for food and family.

I also want to thank our customers and friends who supported me and pushed me to make this book come true.

I'm hugely grateful for the team behind the book. To Meghan Feeks and Ahuv de Chazal who have astounded me with their passion and skill, and in making my book so exciting and colourful. My friend Claudio Caprio who lit up my passion for spirits by helping me to invent our Kimchi Cocktails.

GRAZIE MILLE!

This is my very first book and the first time I published my recipes that often took months of trial and error to reach perfection. I've cherished these recipes as my secret skill until the Coronavirus crisis hit my restaurant operation hard. For a year, we had almost no customers whilst continuing to pay infamous central London rents.

At that point I decided to write this book. As almost no dishes were bought from our restaurant, this book now translates into my dishes being created in kitchens everywhere.

I thus thank you from the bottom of my heart for purchasing this book. You've helped an independent business with ethics, animal justice and human health at its core principles.

You now have the opportunity to do another good deed: Please leave a review for this book on Amazon, Goodreads or your bookshop's website. It will help immensely to promote it further and spread the plant-based health movement. Thank you!

Chef Mauro

Italian and Korean Fusion
WELCOME
HOMEMADE
VEGAN FOOD
ARTISAN
VEGAN CUISINE

FINAL WORDS

You've reached the end of my first cookbook! I am positive that if you implement Kimchi in your cooking, your improved microbiota will have you looking and feeling better than ever before.

On your way to Kimchi mastery, you will probably have some questions or run into difficulties. I'd like to be able to help you with these, so let's connect. I happily answer questions from my Kimchi students every day.

The best way to get in contact with me is via Instagram @vegan_yes. Also, I would love to see photos of your dishes, so use #Kimchi360!

With a follow of my account, you will also be notified of any live cooking classes that I hold, most of them with the recipes from this book.

You can also find me on Facebook by searching for vegan.yes or shoot me an email to veganyes2016@gmail.com.

Thanks again and onto good health!

Mauro